I Am Phoenix
A Kind word to our Leaders

Here it is, rock bottom

An Introduction

from "I'll meet you at Rock Bottom"
It is important to begin at the foundation. There comes a moment in life where we find ourselves at our lowest point, a place where it feels like we can't possibly fall any further. For some, it's the culmination of a criminal lifestyle finally catching up, forcing us to confront the consequences of our choices. For others, it's a drug habit that has spiraled out of control, leaving only death and despair on the horizon—not just for ourselves, but for those we love. In these moments, it can feel as if the weight of the world is too much, and the idea of a way out is nothing more than a distant fantasy.

This is the pit.

The rock bottom.
For others, rock bottom isn't as dramatic, but it is no less devastating. It might be the quiet realization that we've spent the last 30 years living in the same repetitive cycle, trying and failing to produce a different outcome. We wake up one day, exhausted and disillusioned, and realize that this—this endless loop—is not the life we were meant to live. It's the end of a cycle, a life that has yielded none of the results we had hoped for. And yet, there is something powerful about coming face-to-face with this realization.
The truth is, rock bottom doesn't always have to be the final stop. In fact, it can be the strongest foundation for a new beginning. There is nothing more stable than rock, and sometimes, to truly rebuild, we have to tear everything down and return to that solid, unshakeable base. We have to face the truth of where we are and why we've fallen. And from there, we can rise.
So, when we find ourselves at this lowest point, we must not see it as the end, but as the start of something new. The rock-bottom we find ourselves in may be painful, but it is also a place of possibility. A place where, if we choose, we can rebuild, stronger and wiser than before.

Preface
It's essential to start at the foundation. Sometimes, life leads us to a point where we feel as though we've hit rock bottom—a place where the weight of our choices, failures, or circumstances presses down on us so heavily that it seems impossible to rise again. This is the pit, and it comes in many forms.

For some, rock bottom comes through a destructive lifestyle that finally catches up—whether it's a criminal path or a habit that spirals out of control, leaving destruction not only in our wake but in the lives of those we love. For others, it's quieter—a slow, dawning realization that the last several decades have been spent stuck in a cycle that leads nowhere, draining life of meaning and purpose. Regardless of how we get there, the lowest point is devastating. Yet, in that place, there is also a unique opportunity: the chance to rebuild.

The truth is that rock bottom doesn't have to be the end. It can be the firm foundation for a new beginning. Rock is stable, unshakeable, and it forces us to face the truth about ourselves. When all else crumbles, when all we've built has fallen, the bedrock remains, and from there, we can rise.

This chapter tells the story of a young boy who found himself in such a place. He had tasted the freedoms and opportunities life had to offer, but the allure of the party, the lights, the fast cars, and fleeting relationships led him down a dangerous path. At 18, full of ambition, he believed he could have it all—the girls, the toys, the money, the crew, the family. And for a brief moment, he did. But the way he went about it was corrupt. He lied, cheated, and even committed felonies to build the life he wanted, always believing deep down that he was unlovable.

The Bible teaches us that when we sow seeds of evil, we will inevitably reap the consequences. And so, the boy's choices caught up with him, not only destroying his own life but also deeply wounding those around him. His repeated bad decisions proved what he had always believed: he was unlovable. His reckless pursuit of self-gratification left scars—emotional, spiritual, and physical—on everyone he touched.

Rock bottom came for him in a solitary cell. With the possibility of five more years added to his sentence and seven years already hanging over him, he found himself completely isolated, cut off from communication, privacy, and human interaction. It was a cold, harsh, brightly lit concrete box, where only the walls echoed his thoughts back to him. In that cell, he faced the painful reality of his choices, and for the first time, it seemed as though he had truly hit the bottom.

But rock bottom isn't always the end. It's the place where we can choose to stop running and turn back to the truth. The boy cried out to God, the same God he had called on as a child growing up in a poor, alcoholic household. And just like before, God answered. His presence filled that concrete cell, and the boy heard His voice asking, "Why are you still running from Me?"

In that moment, something changed. The walls bore witness to a divine encounter, and the boy knew he had a choice to make—a choice to rebuild his life, not on lies and corruption, but on the firm foundation of God's truth. God, who had always been there, offered him a new path, one built on love, wisdom, healing, and blessing. The Bible tells us that every good gift comes from the Father of Lights. God is generous, and His gifts—opportunities, talents, blessings—are freely given to us. If we build our lives on His principles, we will find true abundance. The foundation of a good life begins with choosing to plant ourselves in good soil, nourished by God's word.

Rock bottom isn't the end. It's the place where the possibility of new life begins. The boy's story teaches us that when we turn to God, even from the lowest point, we can find hope, healing, and the strength to rise again.

In life, we will all face our own rock bottoms. But with God, those low points can become the foundations for a future filled with grace, growth, and purpose. When we stop running and allow God to rebuild us, we rise—stronger, wiser, and ready for the abundant life He promises.

Chapter 1:

The Foundation

A Message for Leaders

Every great leader understands the importance of foundation. There are moments in life where we find ourselves at the lowest point imaginable—a place where it feels like there is no further to fall. For some, it's a result of high-stakes decisions gone wrong, a path that, while once promising, leads to unintended consequences. For others, it's a gradual realization that despite all efforts, life has not yielded the success, meaning, or fulfillment they expected. Rock bottom is a reality many face, no matter how high they've risen.

The descent into rock bottom is often driven by something deeper—self-loathing disguised as ambition or self-reliance. Even for those who have tasted success, there's a powerful irony: at times, the more we achieve, the more we can become trapped by our own destructive patterns. Many brilliant minds have found themselves in the pit, often driven by unchecked desires or misguided priorities. The sad reality is that, even when blessed with privilege, opportunity, and resources, self-destruction can still follow.

In these moments of defeat, we are offered an extraordinary opportunity: the chance to rebuild. As leaders, we know the importance of a solid foundation. And sometimes, rock bottom is precisely that—solid, unshakeable ground upon which we can start anew. It's the place where we are confronted with the reality of our choices, and where we are given the chance to decide: will we continue down a path of destruction, or will we rise again, stronger and wiser?

The story of a man who once had it all—the status, the respect, the freedom to choose—only to find himself in a cold, isolated place after a series of wrong decisions, serves as a powerful metaphor for leadership. In his darkest moment, locked away in solitude, he was forced to face himself. His choices, once driven by the need to prove his worth, had led him to a personal and moral collapse. In the silence of his segregation, one question echoed in his mind: Why are you running from the abundant life that's available to you?

This question is not only for him but for all of us who lead. Why do we sometimes choose paths that are unsustainable, even when we know better? Why do we make decisions that, in hindsight, seem destined for failure? The answer lies in our humanity. At times, even the most capable among us can fall into the trap of believing that success justifies any means, or that we are invincible in our pursuit of achievement.

But at rock bottom, God offers the same message to all of us, regardless of our rank or station: "Ask, and you will receive. Seek, and you will find. Knock, and it will be opened to you." The solution to rising from the lowest point is not found in a new strategy or a different path to success, but in returning to the foundation of truth, humility, and purpose.

Even for those in positions of power, self-destruction often comes from ignoring the principles of moral and spiritual integrity. Leaders are no exception to the laws of cause and effect: when we sow seeds of corruption, greed, or neglect, we eventually reap the consequences. The man in our story had followed in the footsteps of his criminal father, layering his actions with self-hate and creative destruction, hurting not only himself but also those around him. He thought that success could be achieved without integrity, and that his actions were justified. But the result was the same—rock bottom. Leadership requires hard work, but it also requires wisdom. Too often, we operate from a place of ignorance, thinking we know what's best. But ignorance is not bliss; it's the precursor to failure. Leaders must be informed, not just by knowledge of the world, but by timeless principles that guide moral decision-making.

When we ask, If God is good, why do we suffer? or Why are we poor and struggling? the answer lies not in the circumstances but in the choices we've made. God desires the very best for His people, but He will not force it upon us. The abundant life begins not after death, but here and now, the moment we choose to align ourselves with the principles of love, service, and wisdom.

The abundant life God offers is not reserved for a select few. It is available to all, from those on the front lines of leadership to those struggling in obscurity. The key is found in one thing: accepting the gift of Jesus Christ, who came not only to save us from eternal death but to offer us an abundant life here on Earth. This gift doesn't require us to perform or prove our worth—it's a free offering, available to anyone who chooses to accept it.

As leaders, we are called to more than just success—we are called to live lives of service, to elevate those around us, and to build a legacy that is rooted in truth. Jesus Christ, through His life, death, and resurrection, modeled what true leadership looks like: humility, sacrifice, and victory through service. His work on the cross is the foundation upon which we can build not only our lives but also our leadership. There is no greater example of strength than the King of Kings who gave His life for those who did not yet understand His love.

The abundant life God offers starts here. Whether you are at rock bottom or at the top of your game, the principles remain the same. We must build on a foundation of integrity, humility, and service to others. And when we do, the blessings that follow are not only for us but for everyone we lead.

Rock bottom, when fully accepted, stops being a tragedy and starts being a classroom. It is a place of forced attention. When the noise of your own excuses finally runs out of breath, you are left with something few people ever have the stomach to face: absolute stillness. This isn't the peaceful stillness of a Sunday morning; it's the heavy, clinical silence of exhaustion. It is the quiet of a mind that has finally realized it can no longer lie its way out of the consequences.

In this pit, the illusion of self-sufficiency doesn't just crack—it liquidates. You realize that the same mindset, the same "Sovereign" ego, and the same habits that built this hole cannot be the tools used to climb out of it. The internal dialogue you've used to justify your shortcuts collapses under its own contradictions. You are no longer negotiating with life. You have exhausted every "escape," every "fun" distraction, and every manipulation.

What remains is a raw, non-negotiable acknowledgment: you cannot continue this way and expect a different result.

This is where surrender becomes a mechanical necessity. Surrender isn't a white flag of defeat; it's an audit of reality. It is the moment you stop resisting the truth long enough to actually see it. For those at this edge, Jesus Christ stops being a Sunday school concept and starts being a direct response to a desperate need. You don't approach Him to analyze Him; you encounter Him because you require a power beyond your own failing battery.

This encounter doesn't require you to fix yourself first. In fact, it usually starts when you've finally realized you're unfixable on your own terms. There is no longer an attempt to present a "refined" version of your brand. There is only what is real. And at rock bottom, the real you is finally enough to start with.

The "call" isn't a complex ritual. It's a shift in posture from self-reliance to dependence. It is the honest, jagged request for a higher order of guidance.

What follows isn't a magic trick. Your external circumstances—the debt, the wreckage, the legalities—might still be standing there when you open your eyes. But internally, the foundation has shifted from sand to bedrock. A different kind of strength begins to emerge—not one driven by the frantic pressure of survival, but one supported by a renewed sense of direction.

Christ becomes the reference point for the rebuild. The objective is no longer just to "survive" the pit, but to undergo a total transformation of the internal architecture. You stop asking "How do I escape this?" and start asking "How do I walk forward in truth?".

This shift changes the math of your life. Decisions are no longer made out of emotional urgency or the need for a quick "win". They are filtered through a new lens: discipline, integrity, and absolute accountability. Rock bottom, when paired with this surrender, becomes the beginning of order.

Transformation is not passive. It requires that you act differently, think differently, and respond differently to the same triggers that led to your collapse. The work ahead isn't about proving your worth to God; it's about aligning your life with His principles. Each small, disciplined decision is a brick in a structure that won't fall when the next storm hits.

The Pit begins to lose its power. Not because it vanished, but because it has been placed into its proper context: a starting point. You recognize that where you fell is not who you are. The "Phoenix" is no longer a poetic idea—it is a gritty, consistent process of rising through honesty, sustained by discipline, and strengthened by truth. The path upward is no longer hidden. It simply requires that you start walking.

Chapter 2:

The Call to Bring Heaven to Earth

Why must our abundant life begin here and now? The answer is simple but profound: as children of the Father, we have a mission—to bring heaven to earth. We are not just passive recipients of God's grace; we are active participants in His plan. The Spirit of God lives within us, guiding our lives toward the true best life possible. It is not some distant promise after death, but a living reality meant for today. As Christians, with the well of living water in our hearts, we are so filled with love, grace, peace, and wisdom from heaven that we, in turn, offer these gifts to our fellow human beings.

We must treat each other with love because we are all prone to self-destruction. Look at the example set by Jesus Christ—He loved even those who hated Him, to the point of death. What a radical and beautiful way to live! To offer love and kindness to strangers, even to those who might wish us harm. This is not weakness; this is the strength of a life lived abundantly, overflowing with service to others. Service is the ultimate expression of love, and Jesus showed us that it is the key to living fully.

Jesus Christ is the only way into God's family. No additional penance, no fees, no behaviors will be required to guarantee our peace with God. It is through His grace alone that we enter into the Father's household. And with that foundation set, we can now build our lives further.

Here is the good news that both you and I need to hear right now: we get to enjoy the victory over even death. The Bible promises, "All things work out for those who love Christ Jesus." Christ didn't just come to bring survival; He came to bring abundant life. He conquered death, and in doing so, He crushed any fear we might have of uncertainty or loss in this life. Our victory is guaranteed because Christ's victory is complete.

But there's more. While on earth, Jesus was first a craftsman—a carpenter. Before He began His public ministry, He worked with His hands, building and creating. When He was called to service, He set another perfect example: service to others is not just about grand gestures. It's about daily work, humility, and leadership through love. We are like sheep, often uncertain of where we are going, following the crowd without really understanding why. But Jesus is our Shepherd—the one who leads us, heals us, feeds us, and protects us. He loves us enough to make sure not one of us is lost.

This is the Gospel—the Good News.

Jesus, the humble carpenter, showed us how to live an abundant life by serving others. And while most of us won't be called to die for someone else, we are all called to live for others. Just like the soldiers and leaders who sacrificed their lives in service, we too can offer ourselves in service, though our sacrifices may look different.

GREAT NEWS ALERT!

We don't have to die to serve others. We can live for others, and in doing so, we live out the abundant life that Christ promises. We can offer a kind word, a glass of water to the thirsty, food to the hungry, or a moment of encouragement to someone in need. We can wash the feet of the weary, just as Jesus did. We can raise funds for a cause, volunteer our time, or build something that will make the world better. We can solve problems, lend a helping hand, and share our resources. The opportunities are endless.

No, it may not sound glorious. Most of us have spent much of our lives giving others little consideration, offering only our criticism or a piece of our mind. But when we shift our perspective and choose to think positively about others, when we go beyond thinking to action, we unlock one of the most rewarding experiences in life: selflessness.

This generosity of spirit is a key ingredient to living a good life. The rewards of giving and serving far outweigh the satisfaction of being served. True joy is found in lifting others up, not in climbing over them to get ahead. Life isn't just a race t
o

the grave, where we judge each other by who looks the least poor while they suffer. That's not living—that's wasting the precious gift of life we've been given.

Your life has purpose. My life has purpose. And life is truly lived when we discover that purpose. What's more unbelievable: thinking that your life has meaning or thinking it has none? We were created for a reason, and it's up to us to pursue it.

The abundant life is not about escaping suffering—it's about transforming our lives and the lives of those around us. It's about discovering our gifts and using them to bring heavenly characteristics down to earth. There is too much suffering in this world for us to sit idly by. As Christians, we are called to be God's hands and feet on this earth. We are His agents, meant to feed the hungry, clothe the orphans, comfort the broken, and build up the communities around us.

We are not poor beggars on the side of the highway, barely scraping by. We are children of the King of Kings. Our noble blood calls us to stand tall, to lead with purpose, and to bring light to the darkest corners of the earth. If we had followed the wisdom of the Bible, we would have found the answers we needed to live abundant, wealthy lives—wealth in spirit, wealth in relationships, and yes, even material wealth. Our earthly fathers strive to establish a good life for their families, but the truly blessed life comes when we follow the ways of our Heavenly Father.

We have been given gifts—each and every one of us. We can use those gifts to build up or tear down. It's our choice. But the call is clear: we are to use our talents to bring heaven to earth, to serve our fellow man, and to love others as Christ has loved us.

This is our responsibility, and it is also our privilege. When we choose to serve others, we become the reason someone else had a good day. We become the helping hand they needed. We feed the hungry brother, clothe the orphaned child, and give hope to the lost soul.

The Bible offers us an optimistic message. Even if we set aside its authority for a moment, we can see that a positive attitude can shape positive outcomes. Our thoughts create our reality. When we sow seeds of negativity, we reap destruction. When we choose optimism, kindness, and service, we reap a harvest of joy, peace, and abundance.

The good life starts now. The victory has already been won. All that's left is for us to live in that victory and share it with the world around us.

The Mission of the Remnant

We have established that rock bottom is not the end, but the foundation. However, the question remains: why does the abundant life need to begin *now*? Why can't we just wait for the next life to enjoy the peace we're searching for? The answer is found in our identity as children of the Father. We aren't here to just take up space or wait for a rescue; we have a mission to bring Heaven to Earth.

This is not a suggestion. It is a commission. As followers of Christ, we are not meant to be passive recipients who just sit around and soak up grace. We are active participants in a divine plan to restore order to a world that thrives on chaos. When the Spirit of God lives within you, it isn't just to make you feel good during a Sunday service; it is a guide that pushes your life toward the "true best life possible" right here in the middle of your mess.

The Well of Service

If you have met Christ at the bottom, you have discovered the "well of living water." That water isn't just for you to drink so you don't feel thirsty; it's meant to overflow. As Christians, we are meant to be so filled with the grace, peace, and wisdom of Heaven that we naturally offer those gifts to the people around us.

This is where most people get it wrong. They think service is about grand gestures that get you noticed. But look at the example of Jesus. Before He was a Savior, He was a craftsman—a carpenter who worked with His hands. He understood the discipline of daily work long before He began His public ministry. He showed us that the "abundant life" is found in the intersection of hard work, humility, and leading through love.

You might feel like a sheep, uncertain of where you're going or just following the crowd because it's easier than thinking for yourself. But Christ is the Shepherd who leads, heals, and feeds. He doesn't just want to save your soul for later; He wants to lead you into a life of service *now* .

Living for Others

The "Good News" isn't just that we get to go to Heaven; it's that we get to enjoy victory over the things that used to kill us—fear, uncertainty, and the constant cycle of loss. Christ's victory is complete, and because of that, our victory is guaranteed. But that guarantee comes with a responsibility.

Most of us won't be called to die for someone else, but we are all called to *live* for others. This is the core of the abundant life. It's not about how much you can accumulate, but how much you can contribute. When we shift our perspective from "What can I get?" to

"How can I serve?", we unlock a level of selflessness that is the key ingredient to a good life.
Serving others isn't a "glorious" task most of the time. It looks like a kind word to someone who doesn't deserve it. It looks like a moment of encouragement for someone who is still in the pit you just climbed out of. It looks like sharing your resources, solving problems, or building something that makes the world better.

The Royal Identity

We have to stop acting like poor beggars on the side of the highway, barely scraping by and hoping for a handout. If you have accepted Christ, you are a child of the King of Kings. You have "noble blood" in your spiritual veins. This identity calls you to stand tall, to lead with purpose, and to bring light into the dark corners of the world where you used to hide.
There is too much suffering in the world for us to sit idly by. We are God's agents on this earth, meant to be His hands and feet. We are here to comfort the broken and build up our communities. This is the "Wealth of Service."
People naturally want to share their wealth with those who provide value. Money is just a representation of that value. When you serve, you unlock an exchange of value that the world tries to shortcut through lying, cheating, and stealing. But those shortcuts always lead back to rock bottom. The "Right Way" to live abundantly is to serve so well that the world can't help but reward you.

The Commitment to Growth

Rebuilding on a solid foundation requires character. Without character, you won't be able to hold onto anything worthwhile once you get it. For years, many of us lived like rafts being tossed by the current, with no strategy and no foundation. To escape that cycle, we have to grow.

God has an incredible life planned for you, but you have to remain connected to the Source. You have to move past the fear of rock bottom and start moving toward a dream. Fear might get you to stop running, but it won't give you the strength to climb. You need to be pulled by a vision of your best-case scenario.

The abundant life isn't about escaping suffering; it's about transforming it. It's about taking the wreckage of your past and using it to build a future filled with grace, growth, and purpose.

It's time to rise. Let's get to work.

Chapter 3:

The Good Life Starts Now

Say it: I am now living the good life.

I understand that the best life possible is through service to my fellow man, and woman, and I desire to live the most abundant life. Why must our abundant life begin here and now?. The answer is found in the fundamental physics of the Kingdom: as children of the Father, we have a specific mission to bring the order of Heaven down into the chaos of Earth. We are not passive observers of our own destruction, waiting for a rescue that only happens after we die. The Spirit of God lives within us as a tactical guide, directing us toward the highest possible version of our lives today.

This is the "Gospel"—the Great News that victory isn't a distant hope, but a present reality. As Christians, we are meant to be a well of living water. This water is a reservoir of love, grace, and wisdom that we are commanded to pour into our fellow human beings. We treat others with this radical kindness not because they deserve it, but because we recognize that we are all prone to the same self-destruction that leads to the pit. Jesus Christ modeled this by loving those who actively sought His harm, proving that true strength is found in a life of overflowing service.

The Blueprint of the Humble Carpenter

Before Jesus was the Savior of the world, He was a craftsman—a *Tekton* . He spent the majority of His life working with His hands, understanding the integrity of structures and the necessity of a level foundation. This is the map for our return: service to others is not a series of grand, empty gestures; it is the daily work of humility and leadership through love.

The Bible identifies us as sheep, often wandering into repetitive cycles of failure without understanding why. But Jesus is the Shepherd—the one who ensures that not one of us is lost in the wreckage. He showed us how to live an abundant life by serving others first. While few of us will be called to die for another, we are all called to the more difficult task: *living* for others.

This service is the ultimate expression of the Sovereign life. It looks like offering a glass of water to the thirsty, a word of encouragement to the broken, or building a business that actually makes the world better. It is the shift from being a critic to being a creator. When you move from selfish consumption to selfless action, you unlock the most rewarding experience available to man. The rewards of giving far outweigh the hollow satisfaction of being served. True joy is found in lifting others up, not in climbing over them to look "less poor" while you suffer.

The Sovereign Requirement: Authority and Responsibility

Your life has a specific, divine purpose, and that purpose is only discovered when you accept your role as a child of the King. Thinking your life has no meaning is the ultimate delusion. The abundant life isn't about escaping the reality of suffering; it's about transforming it. It is about taking your unique gifts and using them to bring heavenly characteristics—order, justice, and mercy—down to the street level.

We are not beggars on the side of the highway, scraping for crumbs. We are royalty. Our "noble blood" calls us to lead with purpose and to bring light into the darkest corners of the earth. But to reign, we must first learn to serve. The selfish life is the least fruitful path a man can take. We often hide behind excuses: "I'm shy," "I'm tired," or "I'm broke". But these are just different names for "Lack". Pessimism is a trap that keeps us at rock bottom.

The Wealth of Service and the Law of the Harvest

There is a mechanical reason to serve rather than cheat: money is simply a representation of value. The wealth you seek is currently held by other people, and service is the only legitimate key that unlocks that exchange. Shortcuts—lying, cheating, and stealing—are the markers of a corrupt foundation that inevitably leads back to the pit. A Good Shepherd does not allow wolves to thrive among the flock, and unrepentant corruption has no place in a life of abundance.

Jesus taught that to be great in the eyes of God, one must be the servant of many. This is the "Path to Greatness". It requires you to audit your own character and realize if you lack the strength to hold onto anything worthwhile. Without a strategy and a foundation, you are just a raft tossed by the current. To escape the consequences of your past, you must grow beyond the man who made those decisions.

Rising from Fear to Vision

Fear of the pit is a powerful motivator, but it is not enough to sustain a transformation. Focusing on what you fear only brings you back to rock bottom. Instead, you must be pulled toward a dream—a best-case scenario for your life. This dream acts as a magnet, and as you feed it with good thoughts and disciplined actions, you begin to reap "good fruit".

The pursuit of purpose and wealth starts with clarity. What do you actually want? How much money and free time do you need to fulfill your mission?. God did not waste His time crafting your unique personality and energy just for you to squander it. But achieving this requires you to "Escape the Escape"—to stop chasing fleeting pleasures and easy paths. As Napoleon Hill noted, the path of least resistance makes both rivers and men crooked.

True success requires effort, hard work, and focused energy over time. Lack of self-control is the root of every downfall. There is no abundance without sacrifice, and work is the specific sacrifice that makes prosperity possible. All of life operates on a system of input and output: if you want more value, you must offer more love, more patience, and more skill. This is the principle of sowing and reaping that governs the universe.

The Stewardship of the Phoenix

Once you begin to rise and attract resources, you must steward them well or they will vanish. The Parable of the Talents in Matthew 25 proves that God rewards those who use their gifts wisely and punish those who hide them out of fear or laziness. Ultimately, you accumulate wealth not to hoard it, but to give it away. The more you bless others, the more you are positioned to receive further blessings.

You were designed to live abundantly—spiritually, emotionally, and relationally. Jesus said, "I came that they may have life, and have it abundantly" (John 10:10). Your job is to stop staring at the wreckage and start building the staircase. Each day spent rebuilding brings you closer to the leader you were always meant to be.

Take heart. The work ahead of you is your salvation. It is the work that brings you back to yourself and aligns you with the Architect. You are no longer defined by the pit; you are defined by the rise. It's time to get to work..

Chapter 4:

<u>The Pursuit of Purpose and Wealth</u>

All great leaders of thought suggest starting with a simple list. What do you want out of life? If you sat down right now to write out your top ten desires, what would they be? How much money and free time do you wish to have, and more importantly, what would you do with both? Imagine your family life—does it thrive in harmony? Does your spouse or partner last through the ups and downs? And in the best-case scenario, where your purpose meets your resources, how does your mental state fare? Calm, fulfilled, and purposeful? These aren't just idle dreams—they are the essential foundation for constructing a life that reflects who you truly are, a life that aligns with your soul's purpose.

The Creator, whom we keep in mind as we walk through life, wouldn't waste His time crafting each of us so uniquely, only for us to squander that divine design. Your curiosity, energy, and personality were carefully planned. God placed you here with the freedom to either fully embrace the life He envisions for you, or to reject it by living beneath your potential. Some people live only a fraction of the life they could have, while others choose not to participate in life at all.

To truly live in the abundance God desires for us, one must first reflect. Refine your list of desires. Don't simply ask for material wealth or fleeting pleasures; ask for qualities you wish to see multiplied in your life—generosity, patience, self-control. As the Bible tells us, we always reap what we sow (Galatians 6:7). Sow good seeds now, and you will harvest abundance later. Imagine the entirety of your life, and plan accordingly. Live as if the blessings you desire are already yours. The truth is—they are. But you must go and get them.

> "The secret to getting ahead is getting started." — Mark Twain

We often deceive ourselves with shortcuts, trying to escape the hard work it takes to build something meaningful. We chase entertainment, indulgence, or fleeting pleasure, thinking that an easier path will somehow lead to the same rewards. But as Napoleon Hill famously stated, "Choosing the path of least resistance has caused all rivers and some men to become crooked." This "escape" from effort leads us to addictions, laziness, and ultimately, a loss of purpose. Escaping responsibility leads to rock bottoms—whether that be through addiction, broken relationships, or self-destruction. For alcoholics, it's at the bottom of the bottle where they wonder what happened to their lives. For others, it's the endless pursuit of "fun" that leaves them hollow inside.

But true success in life requires effort . Hard work. Consistent and focused energy over time. Lack of self-control is the root of all downfall . Overconsumption—of food, entertainment, relationships—leads to erosion of both character and spirit. It is only when we regain control over our desires and discipline ourselves that we begin the journey toward an abundant life.

The Myth of Work-Life Balance

There is a pervasive myth that we need a "work-life balance." The phrase sounds appealing, but more often than not, it's a demand for more play and less work. Yet, the truth is, work itself is the balance that allows for any life at all . We have to reshape our attitude toward work because work is the very thing that brings stability, resources, and purpose. Without it, there is no abundance—just a hollow existence filled with distractions.

The Bible emphasizes the importance of work: "Whatever you do, work heartily, as for the Lord and not for men" (Colossians 3:23). We were made to be productive, to contribute to the world. When you give your best effort in the marketplace or at home, you contribute to something bigger than yourself. It's this participation that gives life meaning and allows for material and emotional rewards.

A better question than "How can I achieve work-life balance?" might be: "How hard can I work in a sustainable way?" The answer lies not in balancing less work with more play, but in finding ways to make your work meaningful, aligned with your purpose, and fulfilling. There's no abundance without sacrifice, and work is the sacrifice that makes prosperity possible .

Here is where the sophisticated mind must settle. All of life operates on a system of input and output . If you want more money, you must offer more value. If you want better relationships, you must offer more love, patience, and understanding. The principle of sowing and reaping governs the entire universe. If you're constantly cutting corners, giving half effort, and taking shortcuts, you'll only ever receive a fraction of what you could have. Consider this—if you give 60% effort at work, your results will reflect that. You're only cheating yourself out of opportunities. But imagine if you gave 100%—not for your boss, not even for the paycheck, but for yourself. Imagine becoming the person people look to when things get tough because they know you're reliable, you don't quit, and you always give your best. That is the beginning of leadership. True leaders embrace responsibility. They carry burdens without collapsing, they navigate their teams through tough times, and they ensure that those around them are blessed by their contributions. The Bible speaks of this: "The greatest among you will be your servant" (Matthew 23:11). To serve others is to lead them, and to lead them is to live abundantly.

The Game of Money and Value

Money is often demonized, but it's simply a tool—one that can be used for great good or great harm. Money itself is neutral; it's how we pursue it and use it that defines our relationship to it. To attract wealth, you must become valuable in the marketplace. You must solve problems, offer services, or create products that enrich people's lives. It's simple: provide value, and wealth will follow. Once you attract money, managing it becomes key. You must steward your resources well, or they will vanish. And once you've learned to manage money, you must take risks to grow it. The parable of the talents in Matthew 25:14-30 illustrates this well—those who invest what they have are rewarded, while those who bury it out of fear or laziness are punished. The lesson is clear: God rewards those who use their gifts wisely and who aren't afraid to take risks .

But here's the ultimate truth about wealth: you accumulate it not to hoard it, but to give it away . The more you give, the more you bless others, and the more blessings come back to you. "It is more blessed to give than to receive" (Acts 20:35).

At the heart of everything we've discussed is this: You were designed to live abundantly . Not just financially, but spiritually, emotionally, and relationally. Jesus said, "I came that they may have life, and have it abundantly" (John 10:10). Your job is to build a life of purpose that honors that promise. But remember, there are rules —God's laws and natural laws that govern success. If you ignore them, you'll find yourself at rock bottom.

The rules aren't restrictive; they're protective. They guide us toward a life that's rich in every sense of the word. As you move forward, keep these rules in mind. Respect boundaries, both your own and others'. Sow good seeds, work hard, and honor the balance between giving and receiving.

This is the foundation upon which to build your legacy. Your wealth, your family, your impact on the world—it all flows from your willingness to commit to effort, discipline, and service. True abundance is within your reach. Go and claim it.

When you have spent years running, the idea of "abundance" can feel like a fairy tale. You might look at your life and see only the debt, the broken trust, and the exhaustion in your own eyes. But the truth is that healing doesn't happen in a giant leap; it happens in the quiet, steady decisions you make when no one is looking. It is the slow process of trading your chaos for God's order.

The most important thing you can do right now is to stop punishing yourself for the past. If you are still breathing, God isn't finished with you. He isn't looking at your record; He is looking at your heart. He is ready to help you rebuild, but He requires your honesty. You cannot heal what you are still trying to hide.

We often think that to change our lives, we need a massive windfall of money or a lucky break. But real change starts with how you handle the small things in front of you. If you want a life of plenty, start by being a good steward of the little you have left.

Clean your room. Fix the things that are broken. Show up to your job—no matter how small it feels—with a spirit of gratitude. When you do the small things well, you are telling the Creator that you are ready for more. This is the simple law of the harvest: you cannot reap a field you haven't tended.

The Bible reminds us that God is close to the brokenhearted. He isn't a distant judge; He is a Father who wants to see you thrive. But He won't force you to change. He stands at the door and knocks, waiting for you to invite Him into the mess. Once you let Him in, the work begins. It's not always easy, and it won't happen overnight, but it is the only way to a peace that actually lasts.

For a long time, you probably chased "fun" or "escape" because the reality of your life was too hard to face. But those escapes always leave you thirstier than you were before. True abundance is found in the things that don't give you a quick high: discipline, prayer, and helping others.

Helping someone else is often the quickest way out of your own pain. When you shift your focus from your own problems to someone else's needs, something shifts inside you. You realize that you still have value. You realize that you have something to give. This is the secret to wealth that the world doesn't understand—it is more blessed to give than to receive because giving proves that you are no longer a victim of lack.

A New Way of Walking

As you walk forward, you will be tempted to look back. You will hear the whispers of your old mistakes telling you that you'll never make it. When those voices come, remember that you are a new creation. The old version of you stayed in the pit; the new version of you is walking with the King.

You don't have to have all the answers today. You just have to take the next right step. Work hard, tell the truth, and keep your eyes on the promise that life can be better. You were designed for more than just survival. You were designed to live a life that is full, meaningful, and grounded in love.

The road ahead is clear. It's a road of hard work, honest living, and deep faith. It's a road that leads away from the darkness and into the light of a new day. You have everything you need to start.

Trust the process. Trust the Creator. And most importantly, start walking.

Chapter 5:

Rising from the Ashes

You find yourself here, at the bottom, staring up at a life that feels distant, alien, unreachable. You were always the one people turned to for answers, for strength. You were the woman with a plan, the one who never seemed to falter, at least not publicly. But now, you're here, in a place you never imagined yourself to be—raw, vulnerable, exposed. It's hard to breathe in this space. It's like the air itself is different, heavier. You've tried to climb out, but it feels like the more you try, the more the weight of the world presses down on you. It's exhausting, isn't it?

But even now, in the quiet moments when your mind is no longer racing, when the distractions fall away, there's something stirring inside. There's a question gnawing at the edges of your consciousness: "How did I get here?" It's not self-pity, no. You're too smart for that. You know life is more than a collection of random misfortunes. This wasn't chance; it was a series of choices, some deliberate, some unconscious. You've walked into this, step by step, and now you're here, facing the consequences.

But that's not the whole story, is it? There's still time. You know that. That quiet resolve is what sets you apart from others who crumble under the weight. You may be at the bottom, but you're still standing. Your mind is still sharp, your will unbroken. You can rise from this, just as you've risen from other challenges before. Only this time, it's not about proving yourself to the world. It's not about playing the role they've come to expect of you. This time, it's about you .

Imagine the woman you will become after this. The person you are on the other side of this trial is stronger, wiser, and more attuned to what truly matters. What is it that she knows? What is it that she's learned in these moments of darkness? That's who you're shaping now. You may feel broken, but like a finely tempered sword, you are being reshaped, reforged in the fires of adversity. Every scar, every bruise, every tear will become part of your story, part of your strength.

You see, rock bottom isn't the end—it's the foundation. It's where you strip away all that's false, all that's unnecessary. It's where you meet yourself without the masks, without the pretenses. It's where you come face to face with your limitations, your fears, your weaknesses, and, yes, your power. You are more than the sum of your failures. You are the architect of your next chapter.

But first, let's be honest. There are no shortcuts here. There's no easy way out. The road back up will be steep, painful, and grueling.

It will require a level of perseverance that few people possess. But you—you have it in you. You always have. There's a quiet, steady power in you that's been there all along, waiting for this moment. Don't underestimate it. You've always been the woman who could carry more than others thought possible, and now, you carry yourself.

Start with one step. One decision. One move toward the light. You don't need to know what the whole staircase looks like; you only need to know that there is one, and you're on it. With every small step, you reclaim a piece of yourself. You rebuild. You restore. And as you rise, you'll discover a deeper truth—one that's been whispered to you in moments of stillness, in moments when you allowed yourself to feel the weight of your existence.

It's not enough to survive. You've done that. You've survived the worst. Now, you thrive. You rise from the ashes of the life that fell apart, and you build something new, something unshakable. This is the moment you stop pretending to be who you think the world wants you to be. This is where you become you —fully, unapologetically, and magnificently.

Look at the Wreckage

Look around at the wreckage of what once was. Don't be afraid of it. It holds no power over you now. The life you once lived—the one that crumbled—is gone. It's in the past. And the woman who emerges from this, the one who will stand tall after the dust settles, is a new creation, a testament to the fact that you can endure, rebuild, and conquer.

Take heart.

There's work to do, yes. But that work will be your salvation. It's the work that will bring you back to yourself, that will lead you to the abundant life waiting on the other side. Each day you spend rebuilding will bring you closer to the woman you were always meant to be. And that woman? She's unstoppable.

Your journey begins now.

Chapter 6:

Call Upon the Lord

Here we are, standing at the lowest point, where the world feels like it's closing in and hope seems distant. Rock bottom is not just a place of defeat; it's a crossroads, a turning point. It strips away the illusions, the distractions, and the noise. It's where we are faced with the raw reality of our lives and the consequences of our decisions. But this moment, as hard as it is, is also a gift. It is the place where change begins.
There's a truth that must be said, and I won't dance around it: a life without God is not truly alive. It might look good on the outside for a while, but deep down, it lacks something essential. It lacks peace,

direction, and meaning. God is the source of all that is good. Without Him, life is a string of moments, often filled with emptiness, distraction, and regret. But with Him, everything changes. He is the giver of life, the provider of peace, and the only one who can pull us out of this pit.

God didn't create us to stay at rock bottom. He created us for an abundant life, a life filled with purpose, direction, and, yes, joy. The Bible tells us that Jesus is not just a Savior; He's the Good Shepherd, the one who leaves the ninety-nine to find the one lost sheep. Right now, in the midst of your pain and confusion, Jesus is searching for you. All you need to do is call out to Him.

A Decision That Changes Everything

Everything starts with a decision. You might think that it's impossible to climb out of the hole you've dug yourself into, but the moment you decide to reach out to God, everything changes. It's like flipping a light switch in a dark room—the light may seem small at first, but once it's on, the darkness begins to disappear. That's the power of a single decision to call upon the Lord.

When you make the decision to ask God for help, to acknowledge that you need Him, you set in motion a transformation that is beyond what you can imagine. This isn't just about getting out of a bad situation; it's about becoming a new person. The Bible says, "If anyone is in Christ, he is a new creation; the old has gone, the new has come." That's the promise waiting for you, right here, right now. But here's the catch—opportunities like this don't last forever. The moment you sense God calling you, don't hesitate. Act now. Because waiting too long might mean missing the chance to step into the new life He has prepared for you. Ignoring that call will only lead to another rock bottom, one even harder to climb out of.

You might have heard people say, "Pull yourself up by your bootstraps." And yes, there's truth in that. No one else can make the decision for you, and no one else can walk this path but you. But here's the key difference: you don't have to do it alone. God is the strength beneath your feet, the hand that lifts you up when you're too weak to stand. He's not just waiting for you to reach out; He's ready to meet you where you are, right here, in the middle of your mess.

You can save yourself, but only with God's help. Only by calling upon Him can you truly rise, and when you do, you'll find that others will follow. You may not have sought out to be a leader, but once you've tasted the good life God offers, you won't be able to help but share it. And that's how you change not only your own life, but the lives of those around you.

The Mystery of the Future

When you choose to walk with God, the best part is the mystery of the future. You don't know exactly where He'll take you, but you can trust that it will be good. Your greatest dreams may or may not come to pass, but in pursuing them, you will become someone better, someone stronger, someone capable of handling the challenges and blessings that come your way.

The Bible says, "Seek first His kingdom and His righteousness, and all these things will be given to you as well." Your job is to seek Him, to pursue the good life by living according to His Word. The rewards—peace, joy, success—will follow in due time.

As you walk this path, be mindful. The world is full of distractions, temptations, and easy paths that lead nowhere. But you've been there already, haven't you? You know where those roads end—right back at rock bottom. Don't be fooled by the temporary highs of chasing wealth, status, or pleasure. They will always leave you empty in the end. Instead, ground yourself in the eternal truths found in God's Word. It's not a list of restrictions, but a guide to living a life that is truly abundant.

And remember, the people around you matter. They are not just part of your life; they are part of your calling. God often shows His love for us by asking us to love others. As you rise, help others rise too. Be patient, be kind, and be genuine. The more you give, the more you will receive, not just in material wealth but in the richness of relationships, purpose, and peace.

Call Upon the Lord

So here we are, back to where it all begins: you, at rock bottom, and God, ready to lift you out. You might feel undeserving. You might think you've messed up too many times. But none of that matters. The Bible says, "Everyone who calls on the name of the Lord will be saved." Everyone —that includes you.

Call upon Him now. Ask for His help. Believe that He will answer, because He will. He always does. And as you rise from this place, you will discover the life you were always meant to live—a good life, a life full of meaning, purpose, and joy. It's waiting for you, just beyond this moment. You only need to take the first step.

And when you do, you'll look back at this rock bottom not as the end, but as the beginning of something beautiful.

With God, the good life is always within reach. Ask, and you will receive. Knock, and the door will be opened. Seek, and you will find.

The Final Confrontation

There is a difference between being sorry you got caught and being sorry for who you have become. Most of us spend our lives mastered by the first one. We treat God like an emergency break or a cosmic lawyer—someone we only talk to when the handcuffs are clicking or the bank account is empty. We offer a "fake repentance" because we want the consequences to go away, not because we want the sin to go away.

I know this because I lived it. I lost count of the times I sat in the back of a squad car, or stood in a courtroom, or looked at a ruined relationship and whispered, "God, if you get me out of this one, I promise I'll change." I was "saved" a dozen times over, but it was a transaction, not a transformation. I was using God as an escape hatch. I would say the right words, shed a few tears, and the moment the pressure was off, I was right back to the same habits, the same ego, and the same lies.

The Bible calls this "worldly grief." In 2 Corinthians 7:10, it says: *"For godly grief produces a repentance that leads to salvation without regret, whereas worldly grief produces death."* Worldly grief is just being sad that life is hard. It doesn't change the man; it just waits for the storm to pass so it can go back to being a wreck.

The Removal of the Noise

But there comes a point where God stops accepting the transaction. If He has a purpose for your life—if He truly wants your attention—He will eventually stop letting you "negotiate" your way out of trouble. He will stop letting the distractions work.

There is a moment, and it is the most terrifying and awesome experience a human can have, where God removes every obstacle, every friend, every excuse, and every noise. He silences the world until it is just Him and you. In the Bible, we see this with Jonah in the belly of the whale. Jonah tried to run, he tried to hide, and he tried to do things his own way. So God put him in a place where there was nowhere left to run—a dark, cramped, silent tomb in the middle of the ocean.

When you are in that place, the "fake repentance" doesn't work anymore. You can't lie to the One who made the stars. You realize that all your "get out of jail free" prayers were just more static. In that silence, God isn't interested in your promises to be better. He is interested in your surrender.

He clears the field. He takes away the phone that keeps ringing with bad influences. He takes away the money you were using to hide your problems. He takes away the reputation you were desperately trying to protect. He strips you down until you are just a man standing in the truth of your own failure. It's scary because you are totally exposed. But it's awesome because, for the first time in your life, you are actually free from the burden of pretending.

The Point of No Return

When God finally has you in that quiet place, something happens that you can never come back from. In the book of Acts, when Saul was on the road to Damascus, a light from heaven knocked him to the ground. He was blinded. He was helpless. The man who thought he was a high-powered leader was suddenly a man who had to be led by the hand.

That is what it looks like when God decides it's time for you to wake up. He interrupts your schedule. He breaks your pride. He blinds you to the world so that you can finally see Him.

When you have a moment like that—when you feel the actual weight of the Creator's hand on your life—there is no going back. You can't un-see the truth. You can't go back to the "fake repentance" because you now know the difference between a deal and a miracle. You realize that the "trouble" you were trying to get out of was actually the very thing God used to save your life.

Building on the Silence

This is where the "Remnant" is formed. The Remnant aren't the people who lived perfect lives; they are the people who were broken so completely by God that they stopped trying to fix themselves. They are the ones who stood in that terrifying silence, looked at their own hands, and realized they had nothing to offer but their surrender.

Psalm 51:17 says, *"The sacrifices of God are a broken spirit; a broken and contrite heart, O God, you will not despise."* If you feel like everything is being taken away right now—if it feels like the walls are closing in and the noise is fading out—don't panic. This might be the first time in your life that God has you exactly where He wants you. He isn't punishing you; He is preparing you. He is clearing the lot so He can build a foundation that won't wash away in the next storm.

The "fake" you died in the noise. The "Sovereign" you is born in the silence. It is a one-way door. Once you step through it, the old cycles of "getting out of trouble" are over. From here on out, you aren't living to stay out of jail or keep the lights on; you are living to honor the One who met you at the bottom.

The confrontation is over. The truth has been told. Now, the real life begins.

Don't look back. There is nothing left for you there anyway. Look at the One who finally has your attention, and ask Him what the next step is. He's been waiting a long time for you to finally be quiet enough to hear the answer.

About the Author

About the Author

Alexander Dalgardno is a writer, builder, and creator (<u>Pen name and Social Media Character Alx Luxmanov</u>) whose work centers on transformation, responsibility, and the process of rebuilding a life from its lowest point into something stable, disciplined, and meaningful. His perspective is not shaped by abstract theory alone, but by lived experience—moments of loss, reflection, correction, and gradual reconstruction. Rather than presenting himself as someone who has arrived at a final destination, he writes as someone who has committed himself to a direction: continual growth, alignment, and the pursuit of a life that reflects truth over illusion.

At the core of Alexander's work is a simple but demanding idea: people are not defined by where they fall, but by what they choose to do once they become aware of where they stand. This belief is not presented as motivational language, but as a practical framework for change. His writing emphasizes clarity over comfort, ownership over avoidance, and action over passive intention. The goal is not to inspire temporary emotion, but to provoke a lasting shift in how a person sees themselves and their circumstances.

Alexander's work is closely tied to the development of LXMNV, a platform and body of ideas that reflects his broader philosophy. LXMNV represents more than a brand—it is an evolving expression of his approach to personal development, value creation, and sovereignty. Through this platform, he explores what it means to build something meaningful from the ground up, both internally and externally. The emphasis is not simply on success in a material sense, but on becoming someone capable of sustaining success through discipline, integrity, and consistency.

The ideas presented through LXMNV and his writing often revolve around the relationship between mindset and behavior. Alexander highlights the importance of recognizing patterns—particularly the cycles that keep individuals stagnant or disconnected from their potential. He approaches these patterns not as moral failures, but as systems that can be understood, analyzed, and ultimately changed. This analytical perspective allows his work to remain grounded in reality, rather than drifting into vague or purely inspirational messaging.

While his tone can be direct and at times confrontational, it is intentional. Alexander's writing is designed to challenge the reader to move beyond passive consumption and into active reflection. He does not position himself as a distant authority speaking from above, but as someone speaking alongside the reader—someone who understands the difficulty of change and the resistance that often accompanies it. His aim is not to overwhelm, but to clarify. Not to impress, but to reveal. Faith plays a meaningful role in his worldview, though it is expressed in a way that emphasizes personal responsibility and internal alignment rather than performance or outward appearance. His perspective integrates the idea that transformation involves more than just external change; it requires a shift in identity, priorities, and habits. This internal transformation is seen as the foundation upon which everything else is built. Without it, progress tends to be temporary or unstable.

Alexander's approach to writing reflects this philosophy. His work often blends narrative elements with structured thought, allowing readers to engage both emotionally and intellectually. Stories and lived moments are used not as decoration, but as anchors that make abstract principles more tangible. By connecting ideas to real experiences, he aims to create a sense of relatability that encourages the reader to see their own life through a clearer lens.

In addition to his written work, Alexander maintains a presence across digital platforms where he shares ideas, reflections, and perspectives that align with his broader message. His content often explores themes such as discipline, accountability, purpose, and the process of rebuilding from difficult circumstances. While the formats may vary, the underlying intention remains consistent: to communicate ideas that help individuals take ownership of their lives and begin moving in a more deliberate direction.

A recurring theme throughout Alexander's work is the concept of starting from where you are, rather than where you wish you were. This principle is central to his philosophy. It acknowledges that many people delay meaningful change because they are waiting for the "right" conditions, the "right" timing, or the "right" version of themselves to emerge. His perspective challenges this delay by emphasizing that progress begins with honest assessment. Once a person understands their current position without distortion, they are better equipped to take meaningful steps forward.

Another key aspect of his message is the importance of consistency over intensity. While moments of motivation can spark change, they are not sufficient to sustain it. Alexander emphasizes that lasting transformation is built through repeated actions over time, even when those actions are difficult or unremarkable. This focus on process rather than outcome helps shift attention away from short-term thinking and toward long-term development.

His work also touches on the idea of value—both in terms of what an individual contributes to others and how they perceive their own worth. Rather than framing value as something external or dependent solely on achievement, he presents it as something that is cultivated through discipline, skill, and the willingness to improve. In this view, value is not static; it evolves as a person grows and takes responsibility for their actions and decisions.

Through LXMNV and his broader creative efforts, Alexander continues to develop a framework that combines philosophy, practical guidance, and personal reflection. His work is not presented as a rigid system with fixed outcomes, but as a flexible approach that individuals can adapt to their own circumstances. The underlying principles remain consistent, but the application varies depending on the person and their situation.

Alexander's writing is often aimed at those who find themselves at a turning point—individuals who recognize that their current path is not aligned with the life they want to build. For these readers, his work serves as both a challenge and a guide. It challenges assumptions, questions excuses, and encourages honesty. At the same time, it offers a way forward that is grounded in actionable steps and realistic expectations.

Rather than focusing on perfection, his message emphasizes progress. Rather than promoting comparison, it encourages self-awareness. And rather than offering quick fixes, it highlights the importance of long-term commitment. These themes are consistent across his work and reflect his belief that meaningful change requires both clarity of thought and discipline in execution.

In many ways, Alexander's perspective is shaped by the understanding that growth is not linear. Setbacks, uncertainty, and moments of doubt are part of the process. His writing acknowledges these realities without framing them as reasons to stop, but rather as conditions to navigate. This honest approach allows readers to engage with his work in a way that feels grounded and applicable, rather than idealistic or disconnected from real life.

Ultimately, Alexander Dalgardno's work is centered on a simple but powerful idea: that individuals have the capacity to change their trajectory if they are willing to confront reality, take responsibility, and commit to the process of rebuilding. Through his writing, platforms, and ongoing projects, he continues to explore and communicate this idea, offering a perspective that blends personal experience with practical insight.

He does not claim to have all the answers, nor does he present himself as someone who has completed the journey. Instead, his work reflects an ongoing commitment to the path itself—a path defined by learning, adjusting, and moving forward with intention. For those who encounter his writing, the invitation is not to admire from a distance, but to reflect, evaluate, and decide what direction they are willing to take in their own lives.

At its foundation, his message remains consistent:

Clarity leads to awareness.

Awareness leads to responsibility.

Responsibility leads to change.
And change, sustained over time, leads to a different life.
That is the principle guiding his work—and the perspective he continues to build upon.

www.ingramcontent.com/pod-product-compliance
Lightning Source LLC
Chambersburg PA
CBHW030519220526
45464CB00006B/2867